HAND-LETTERED FROM A-Z

an ALPHABET COLORING BOOK

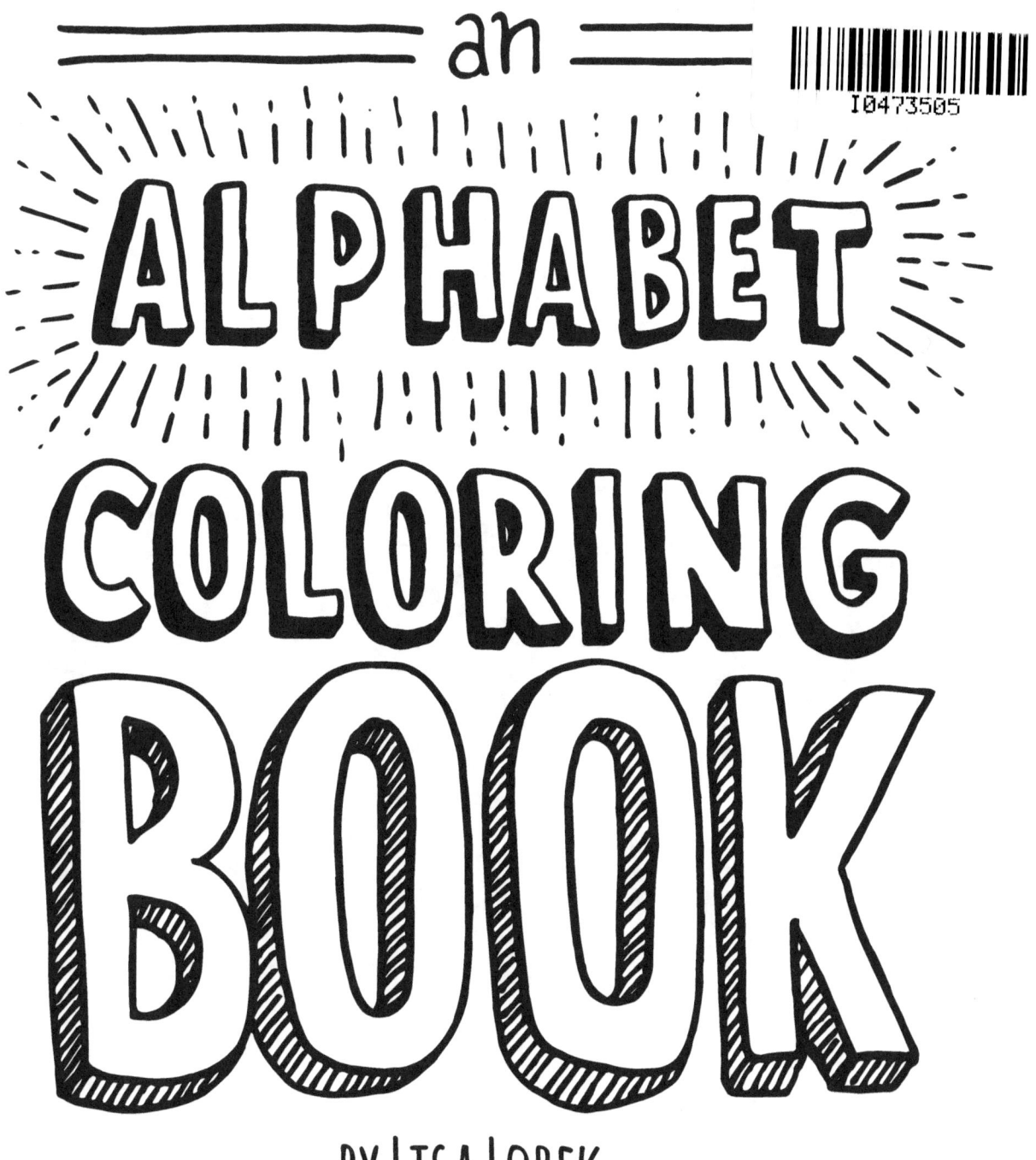

by Lisa Lorek

Copyright © 2015 Lisa Lorek

Published by Free Period Press
www.freeperiodpress.com

ISBN 978-0-9909144-1-9

I0473505

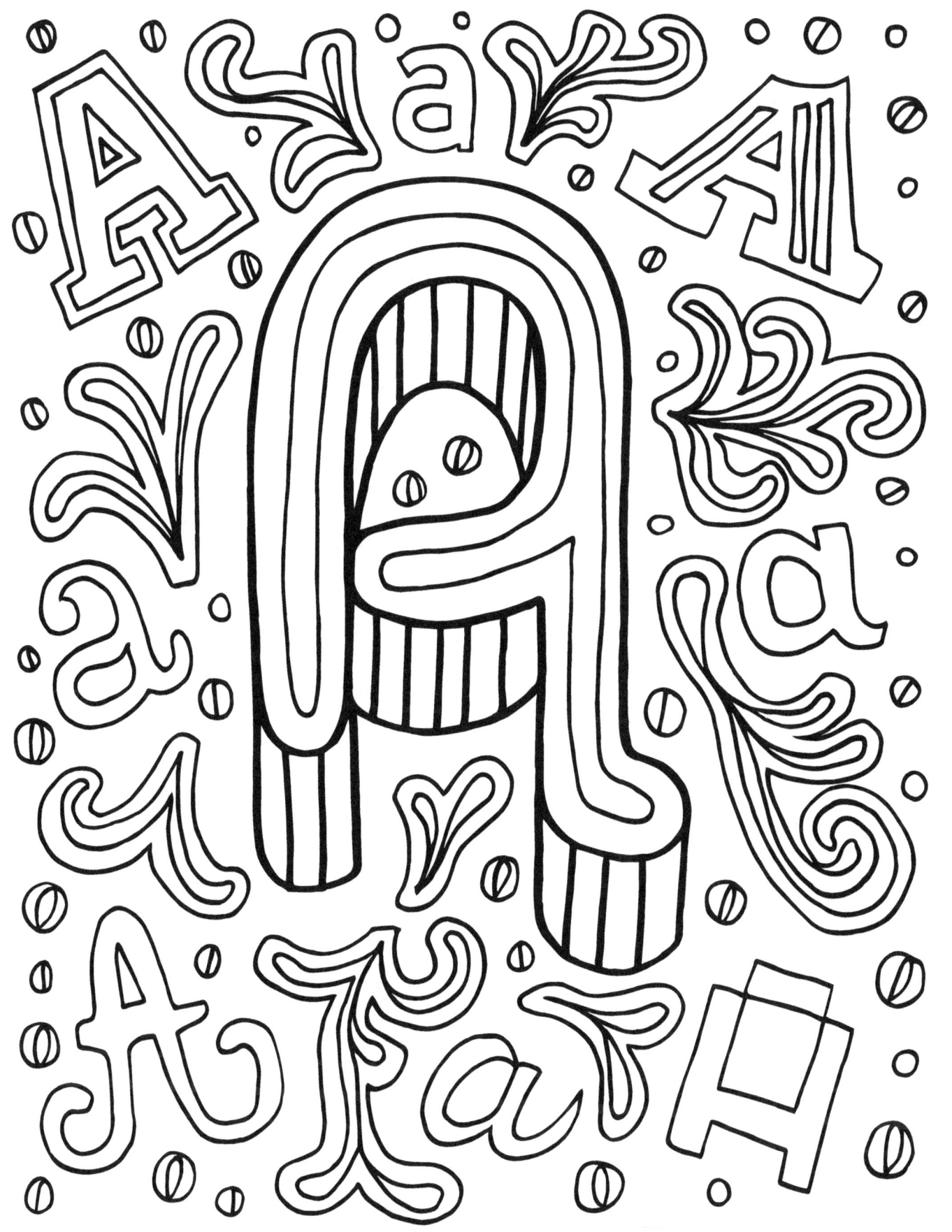

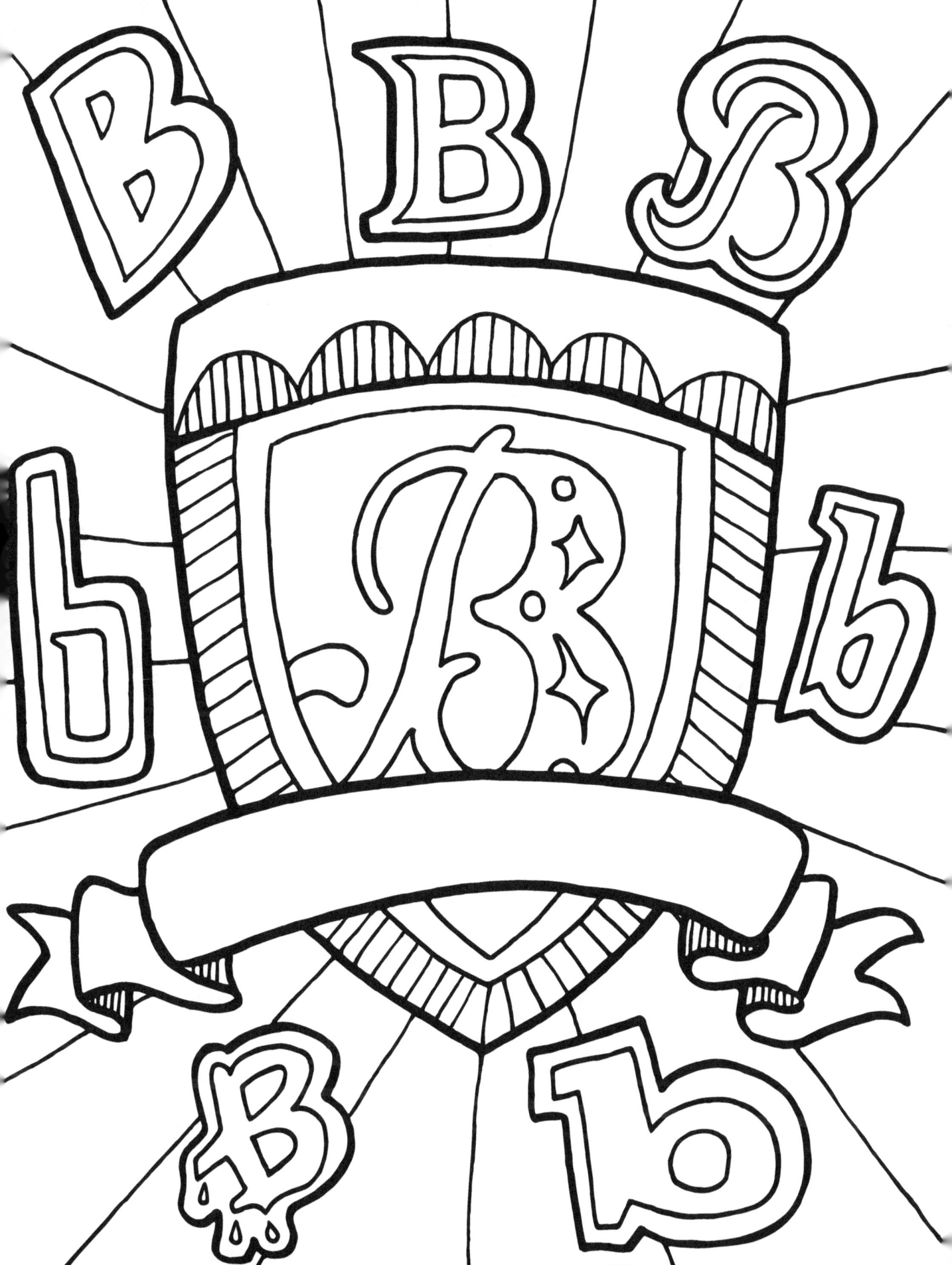

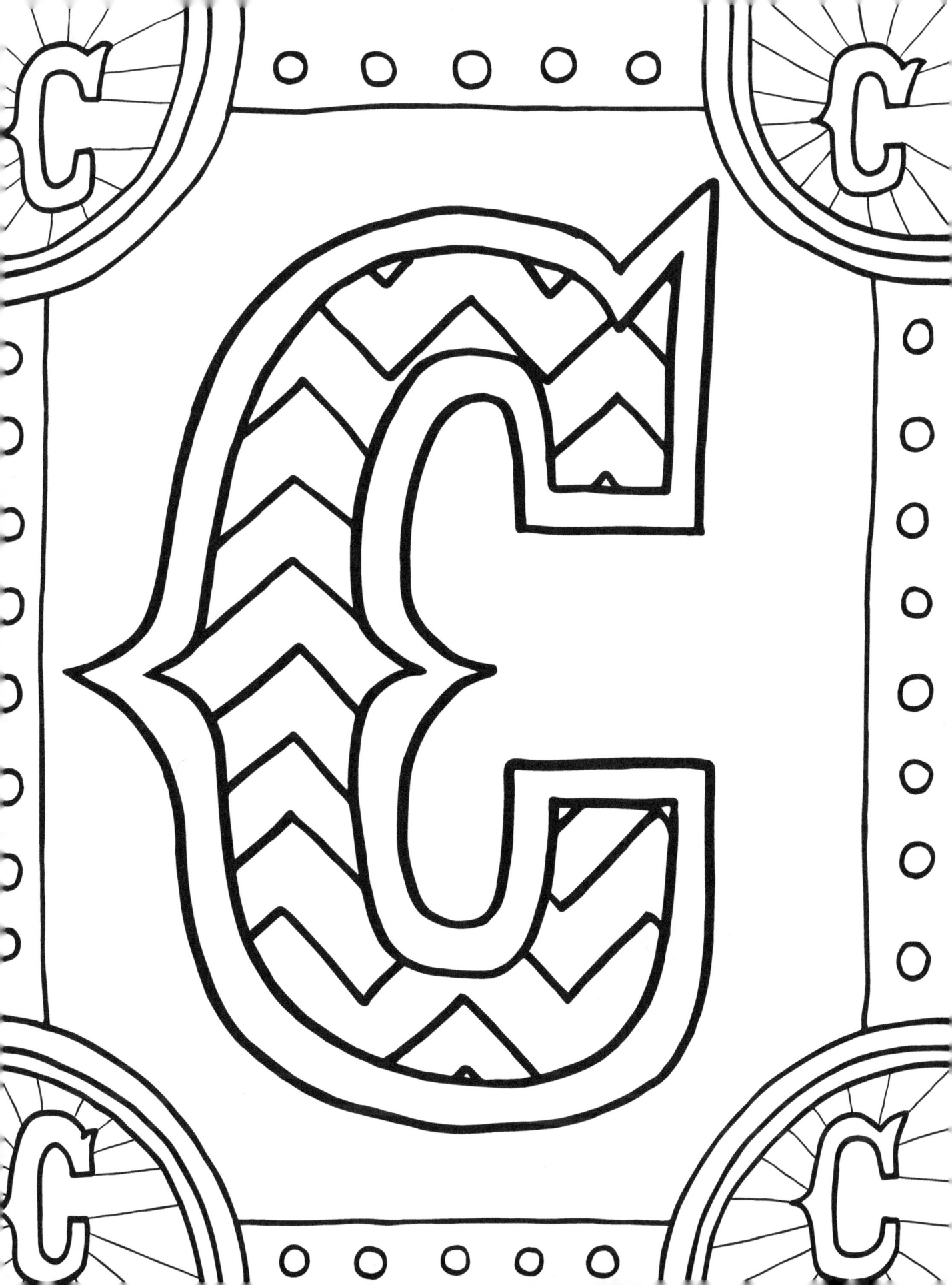

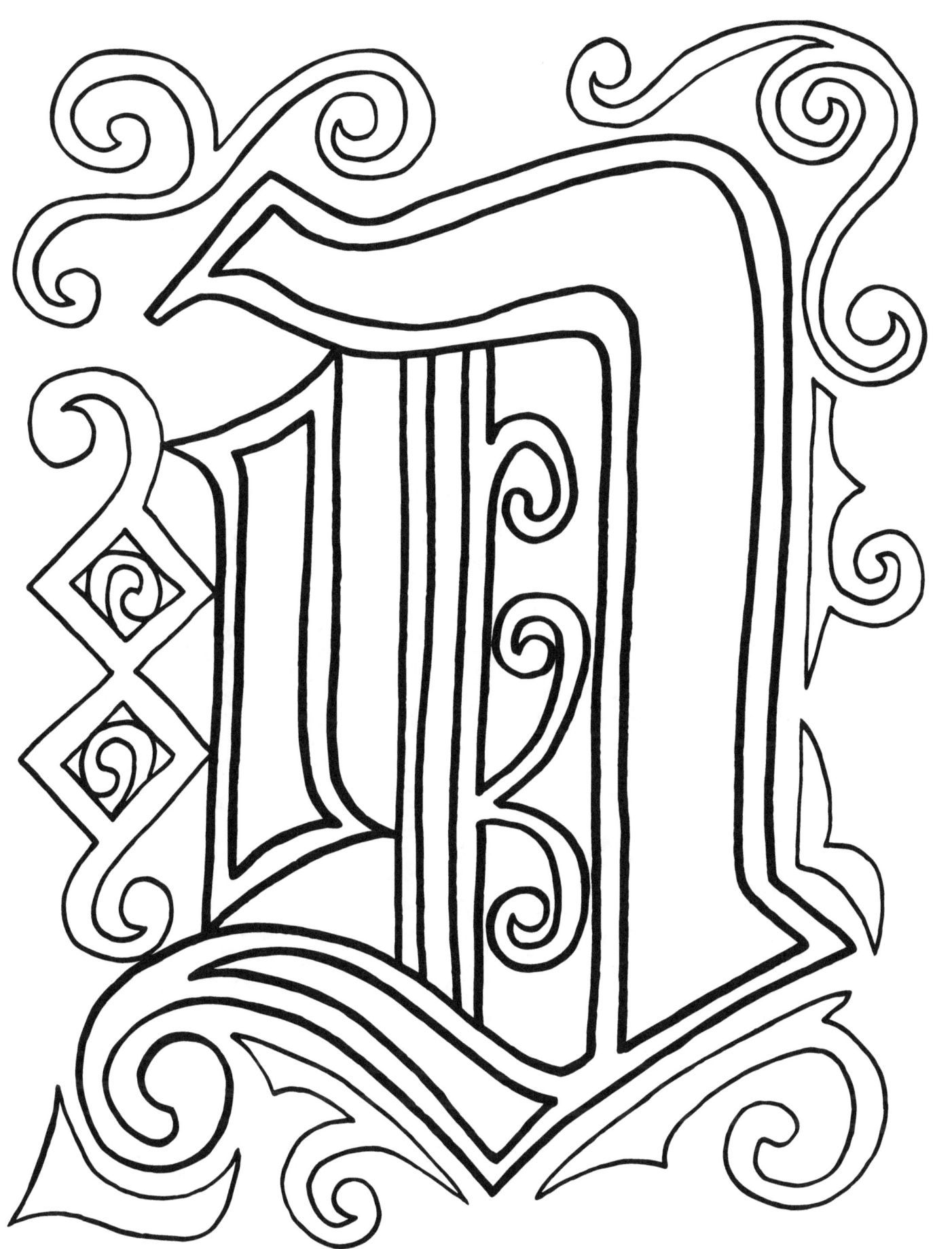

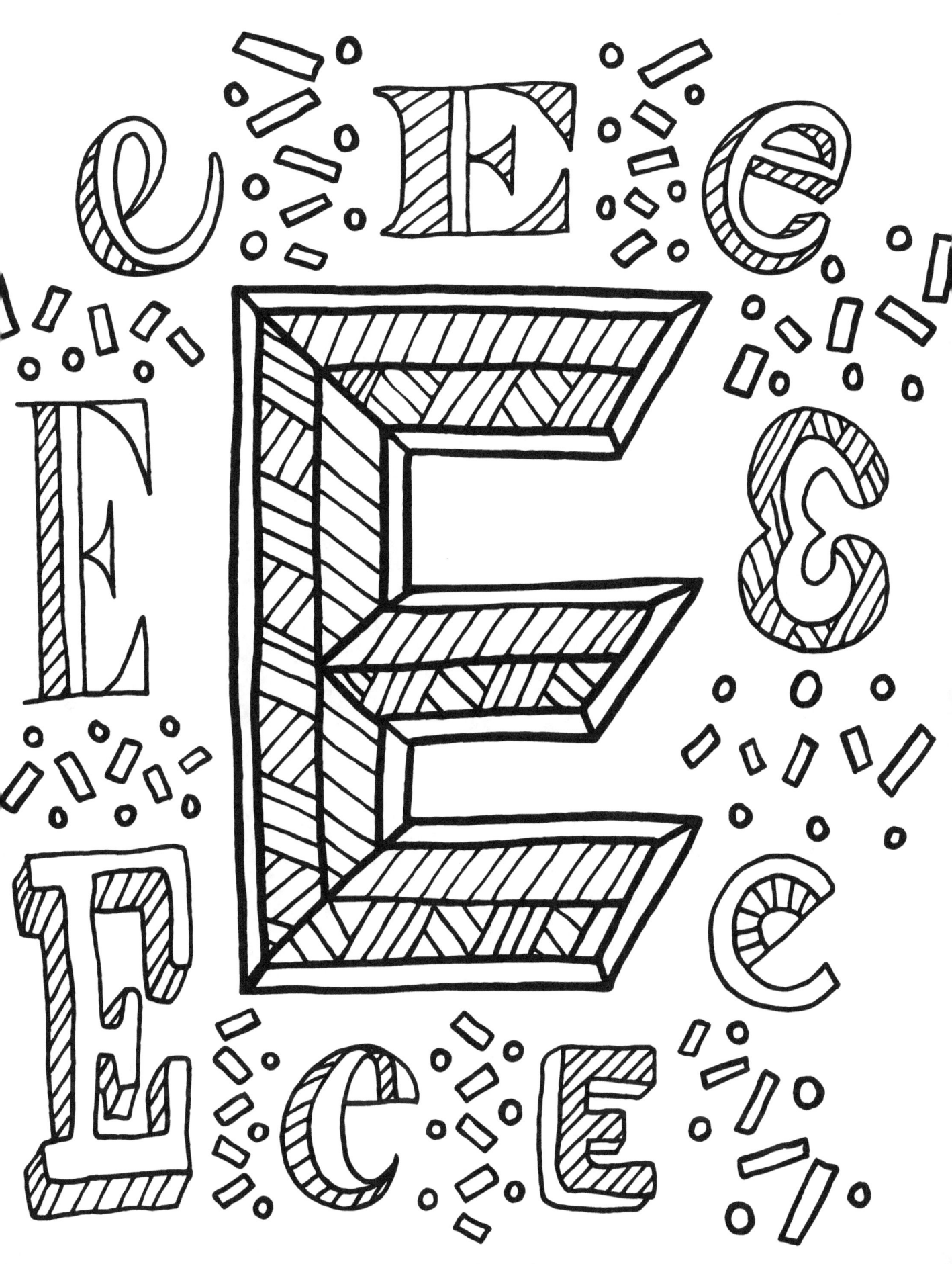

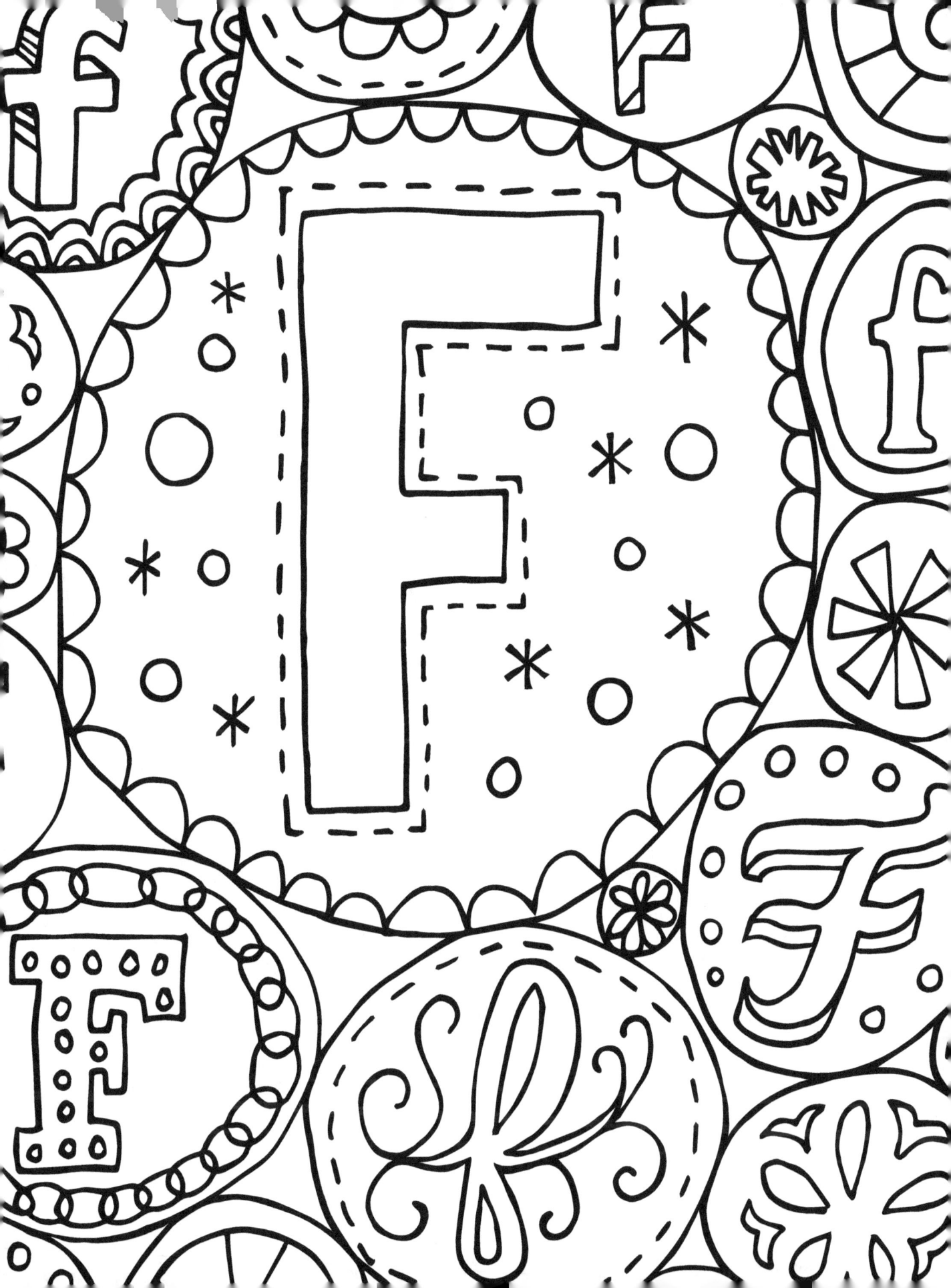

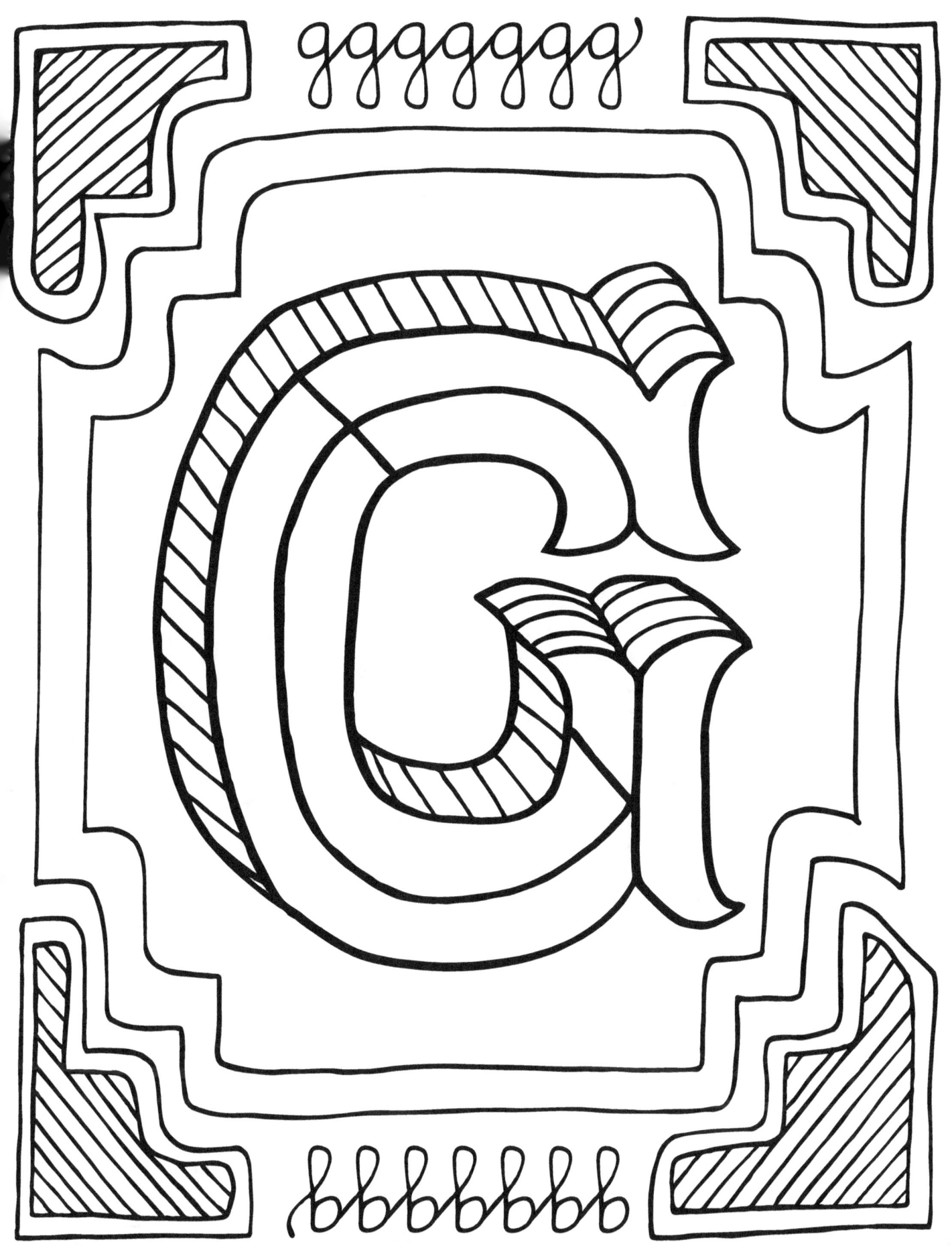

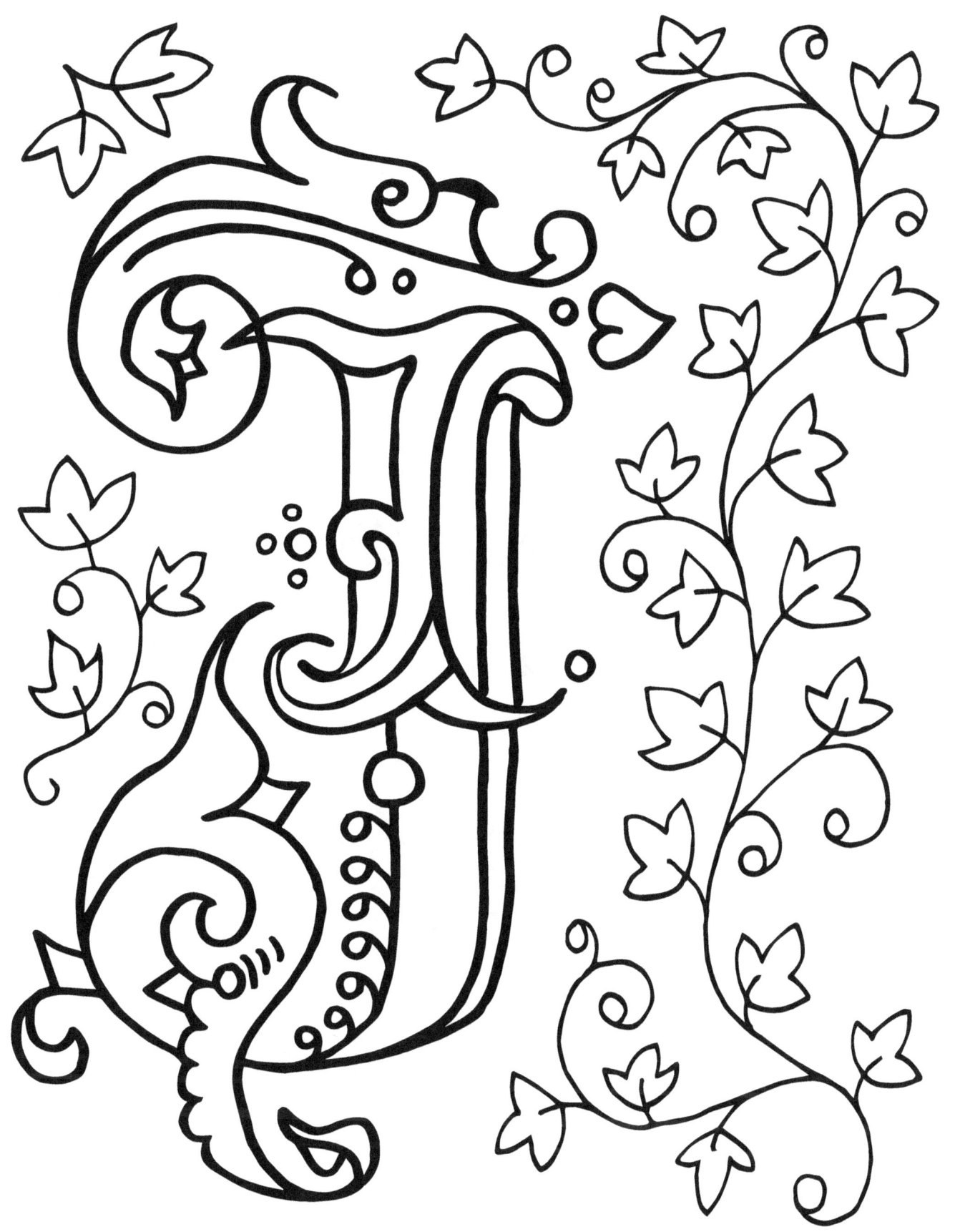

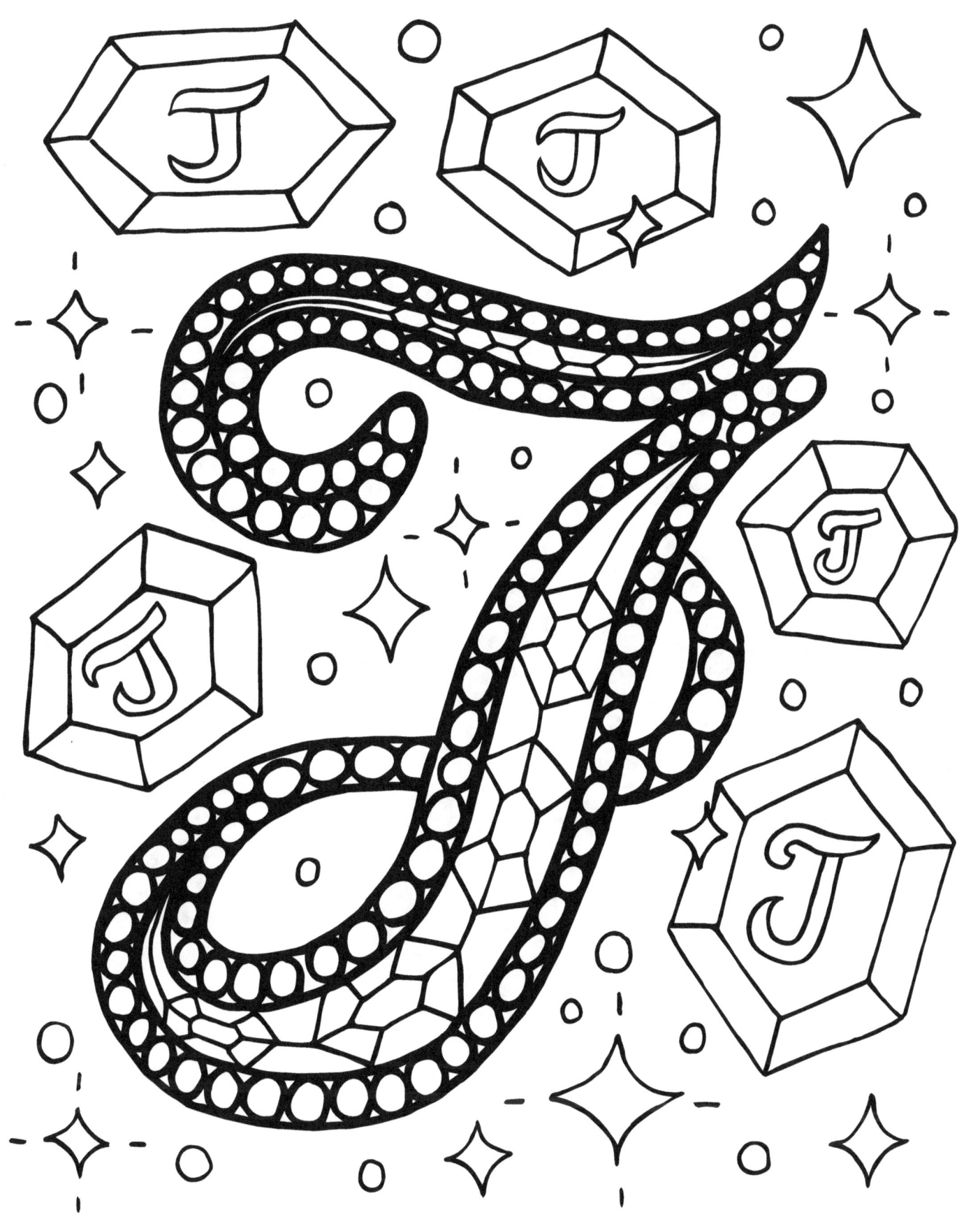

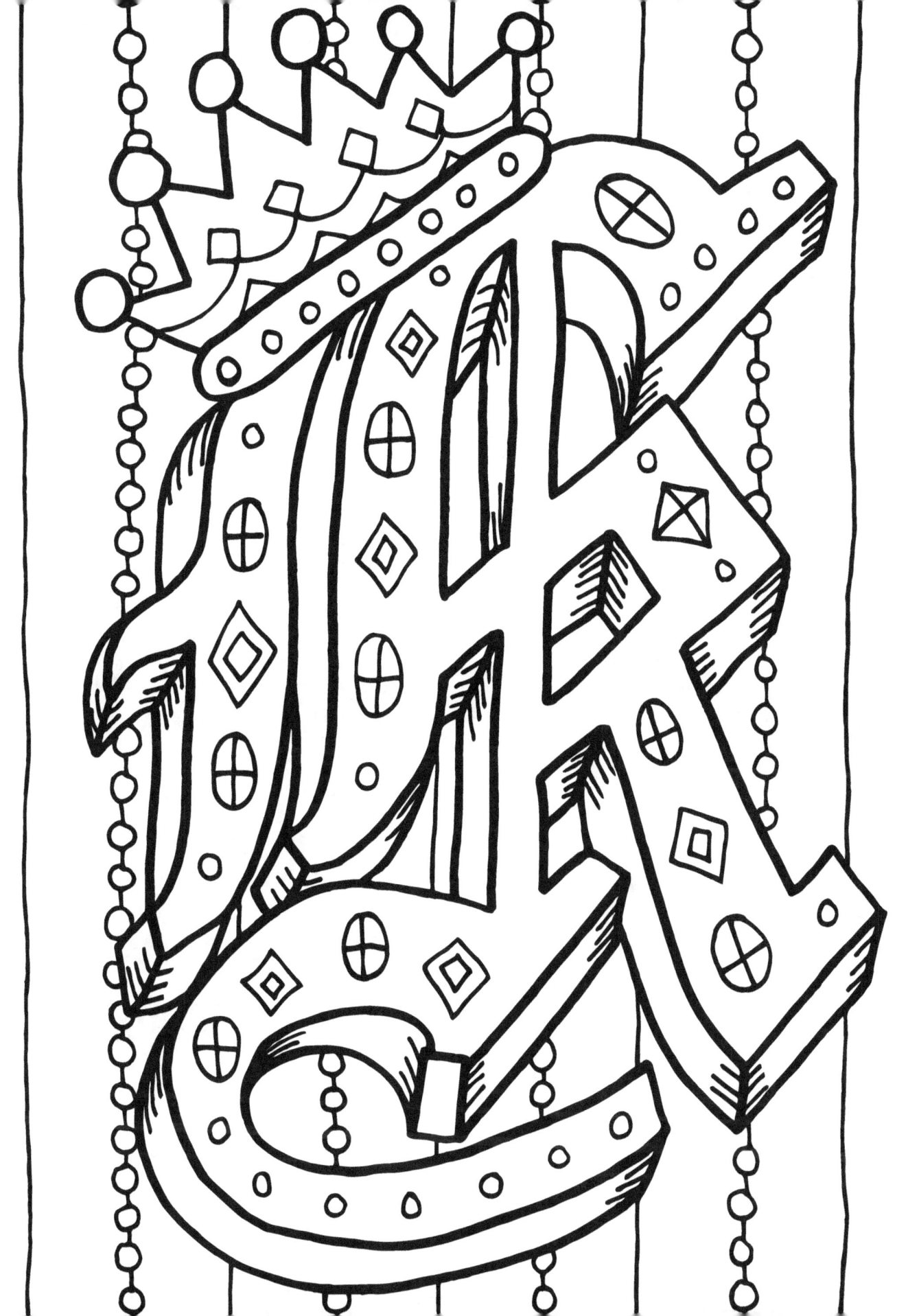

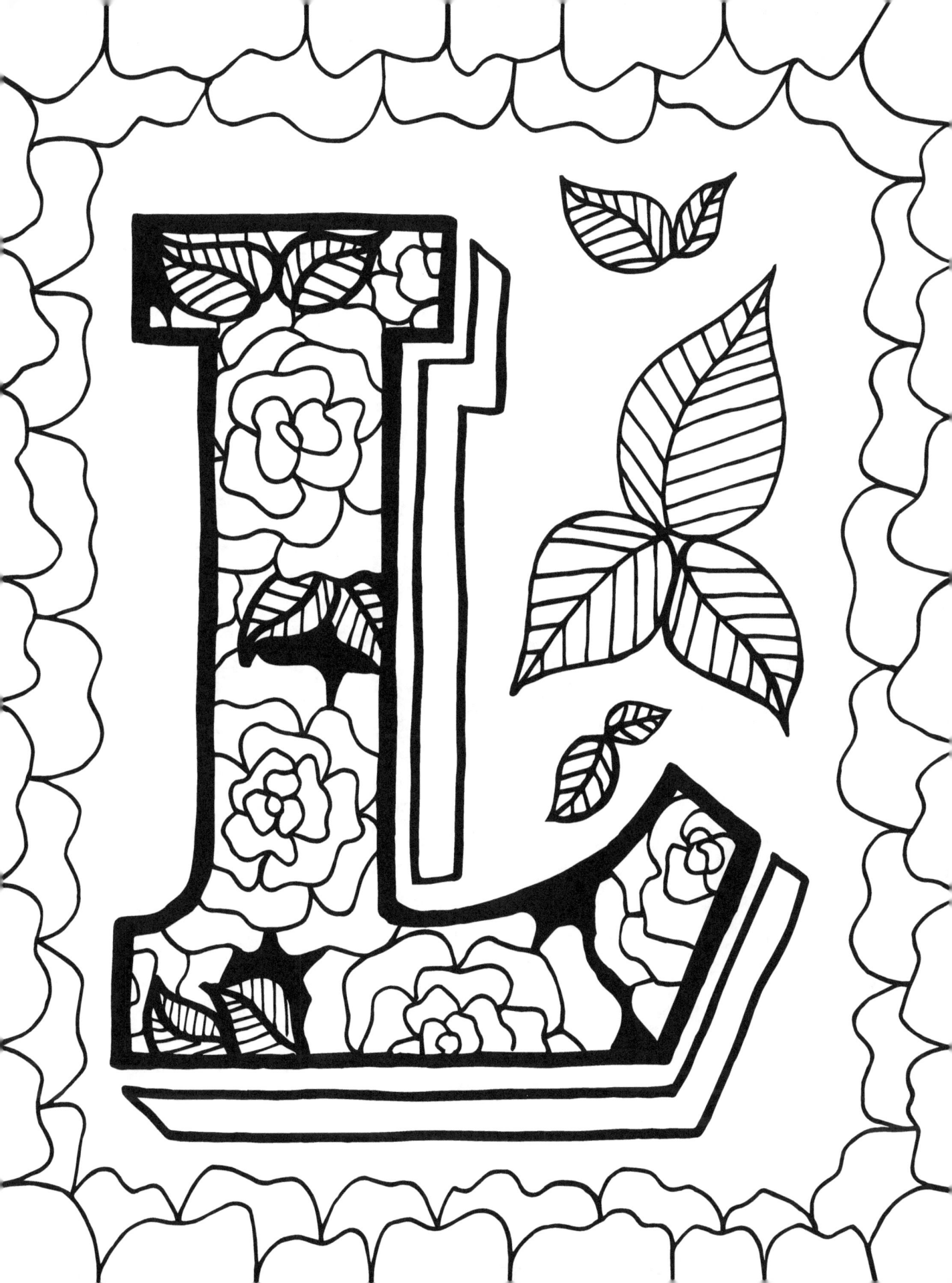

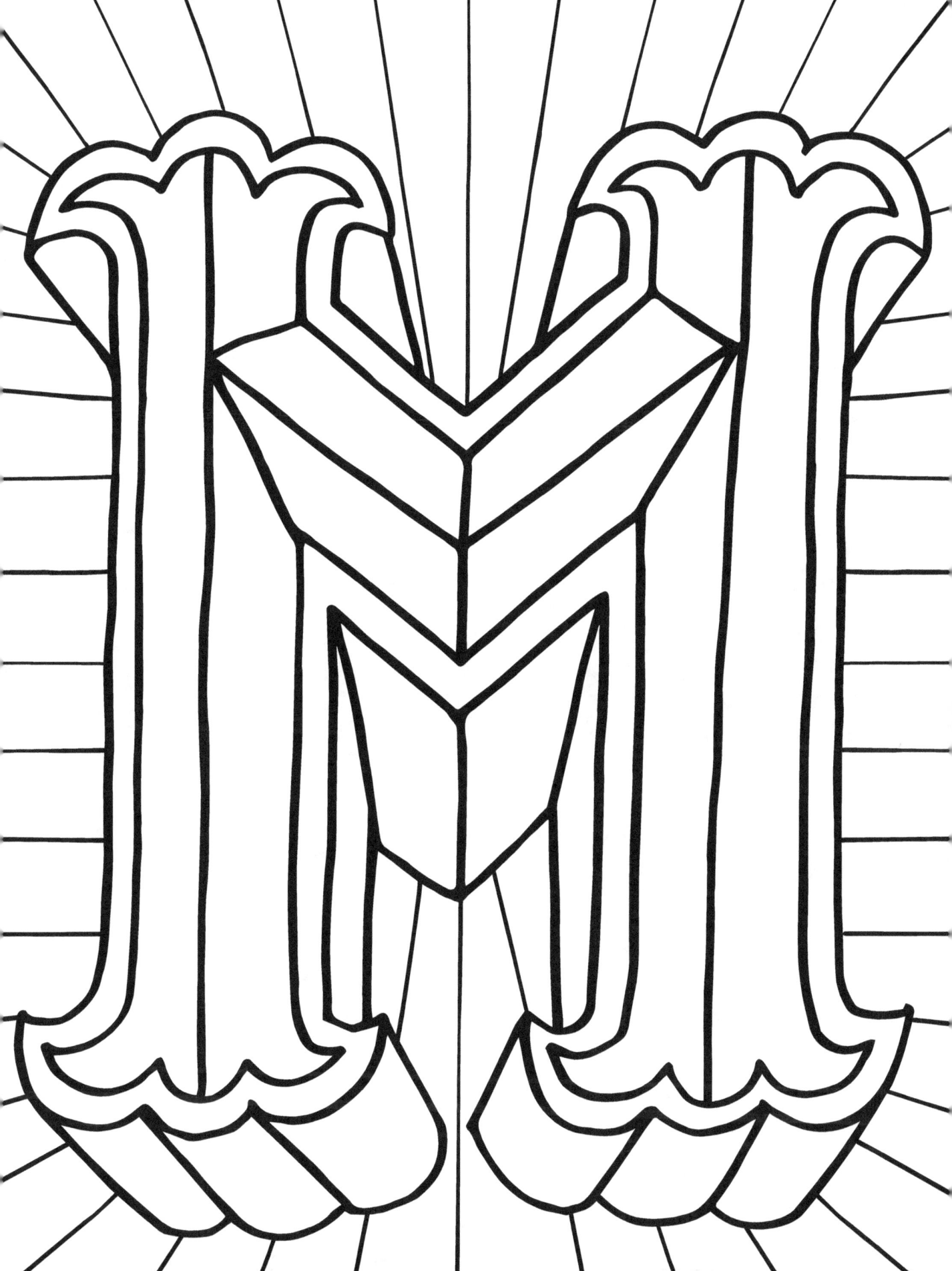

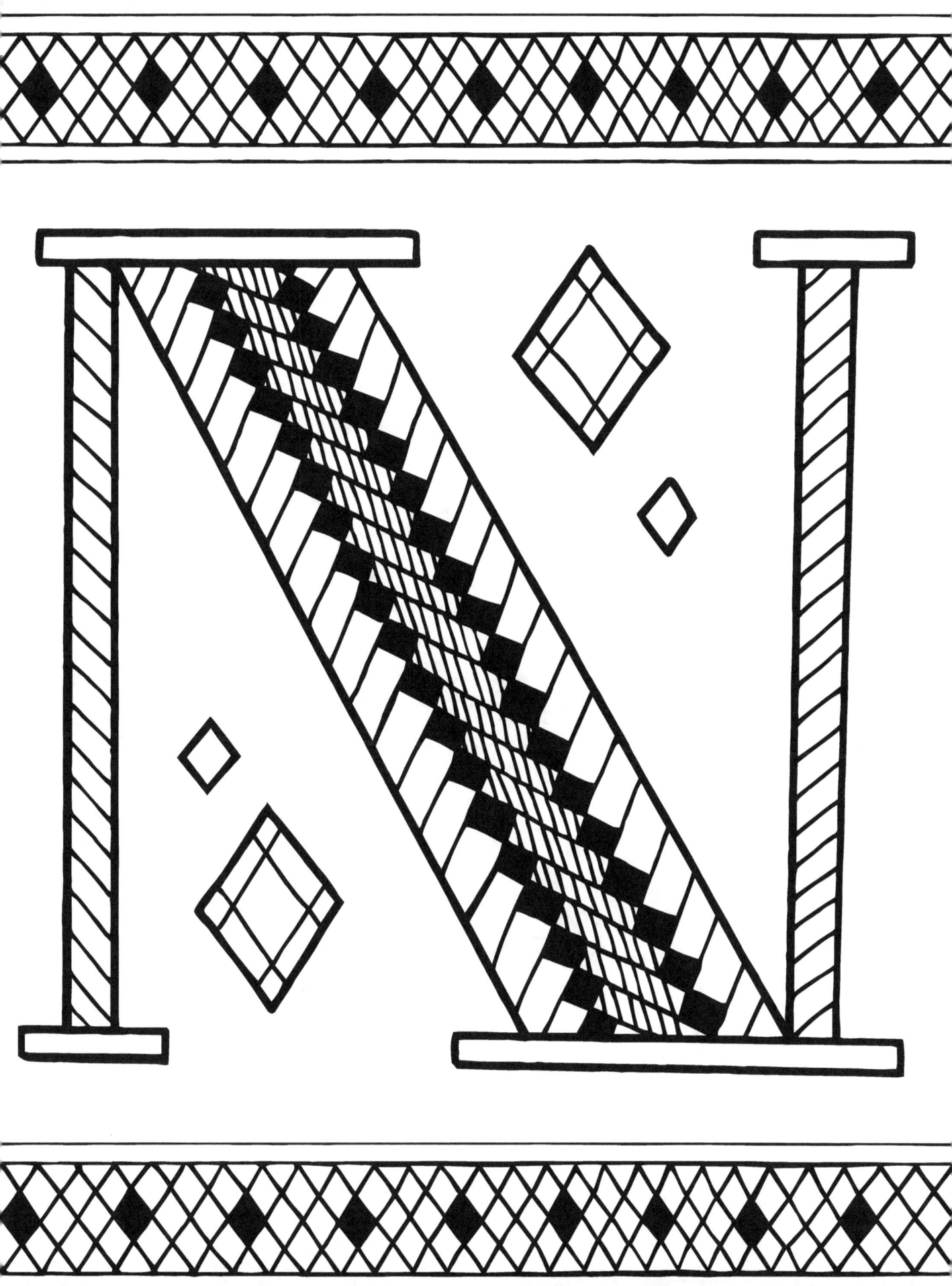

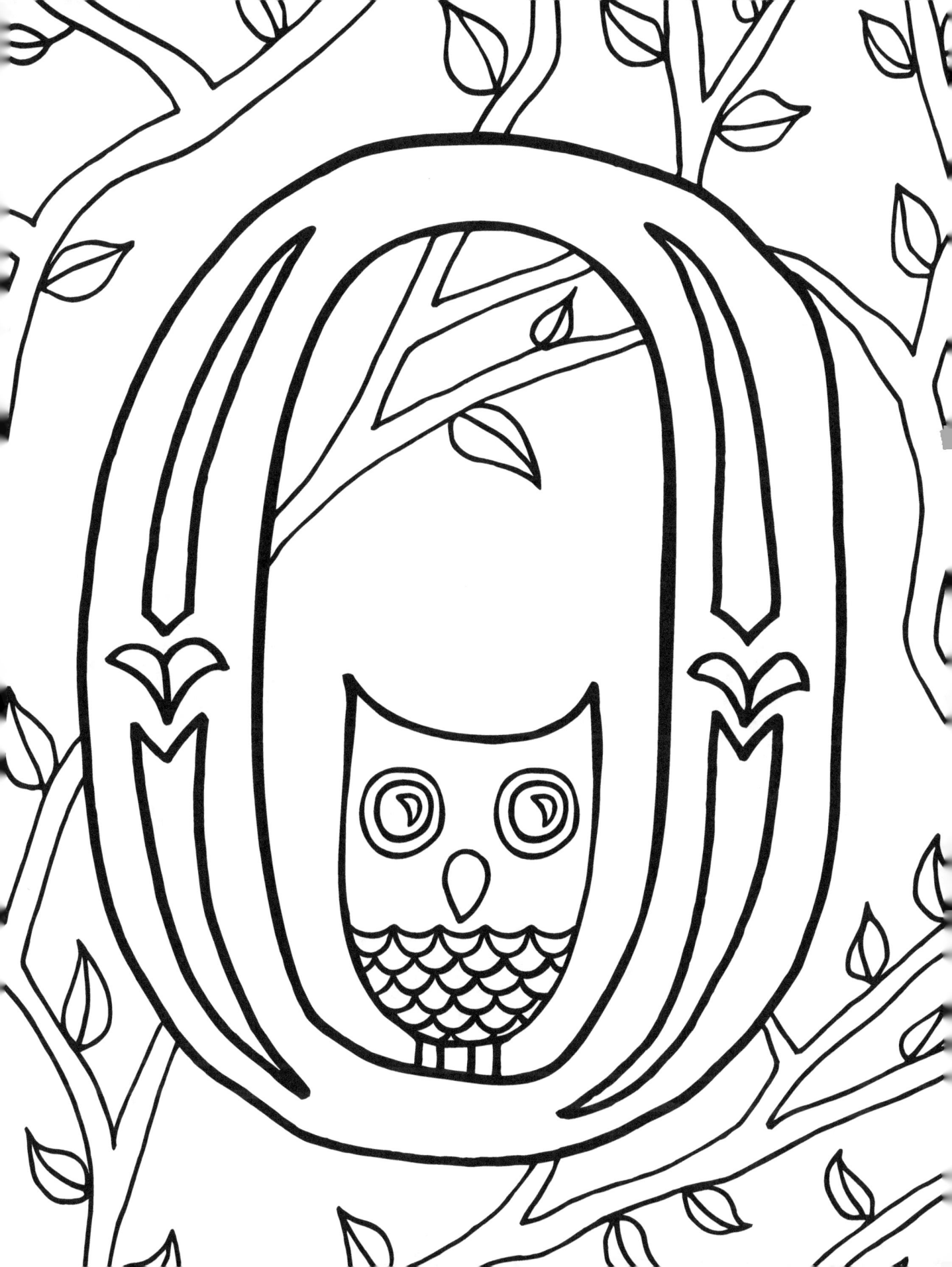

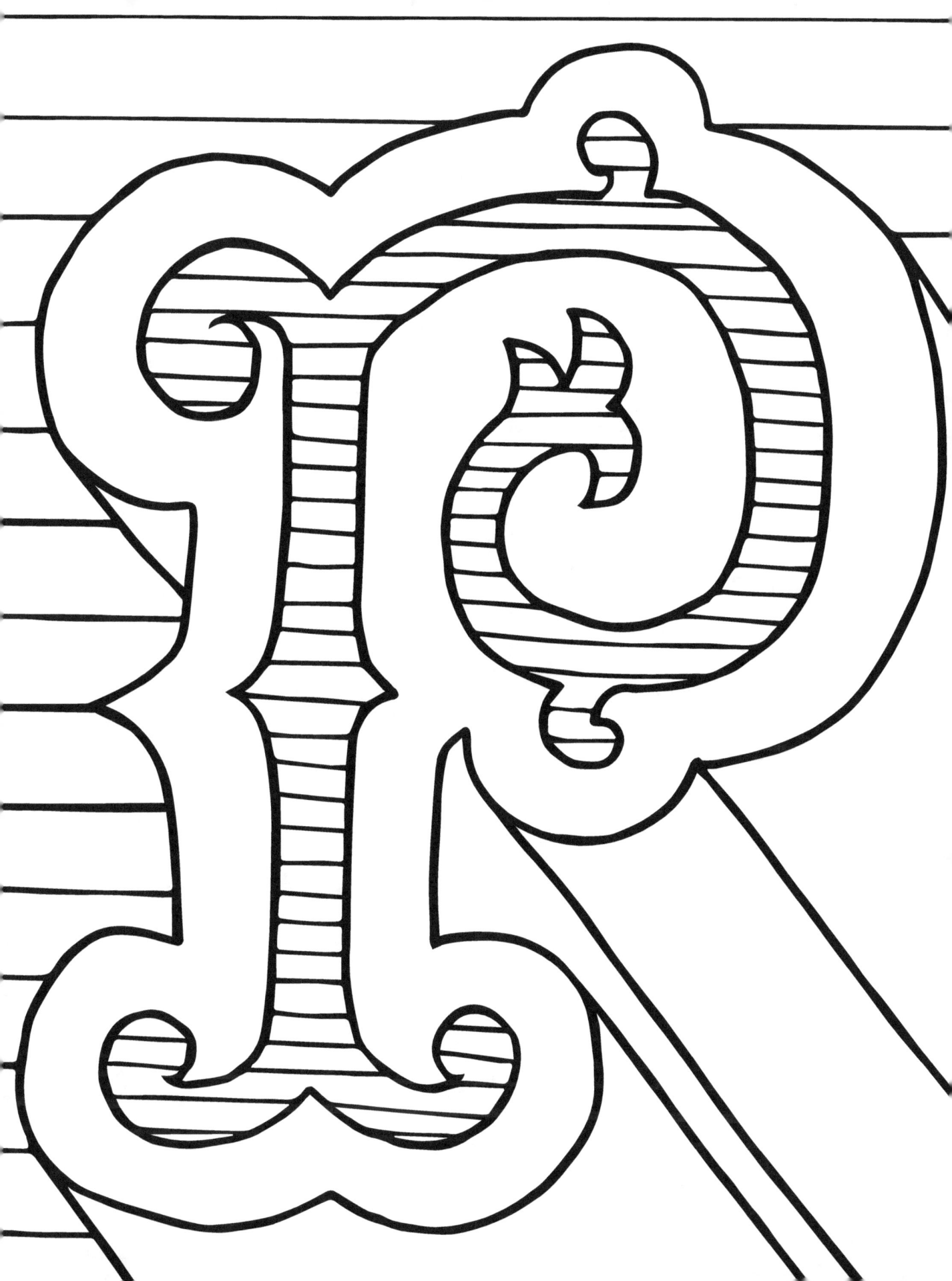

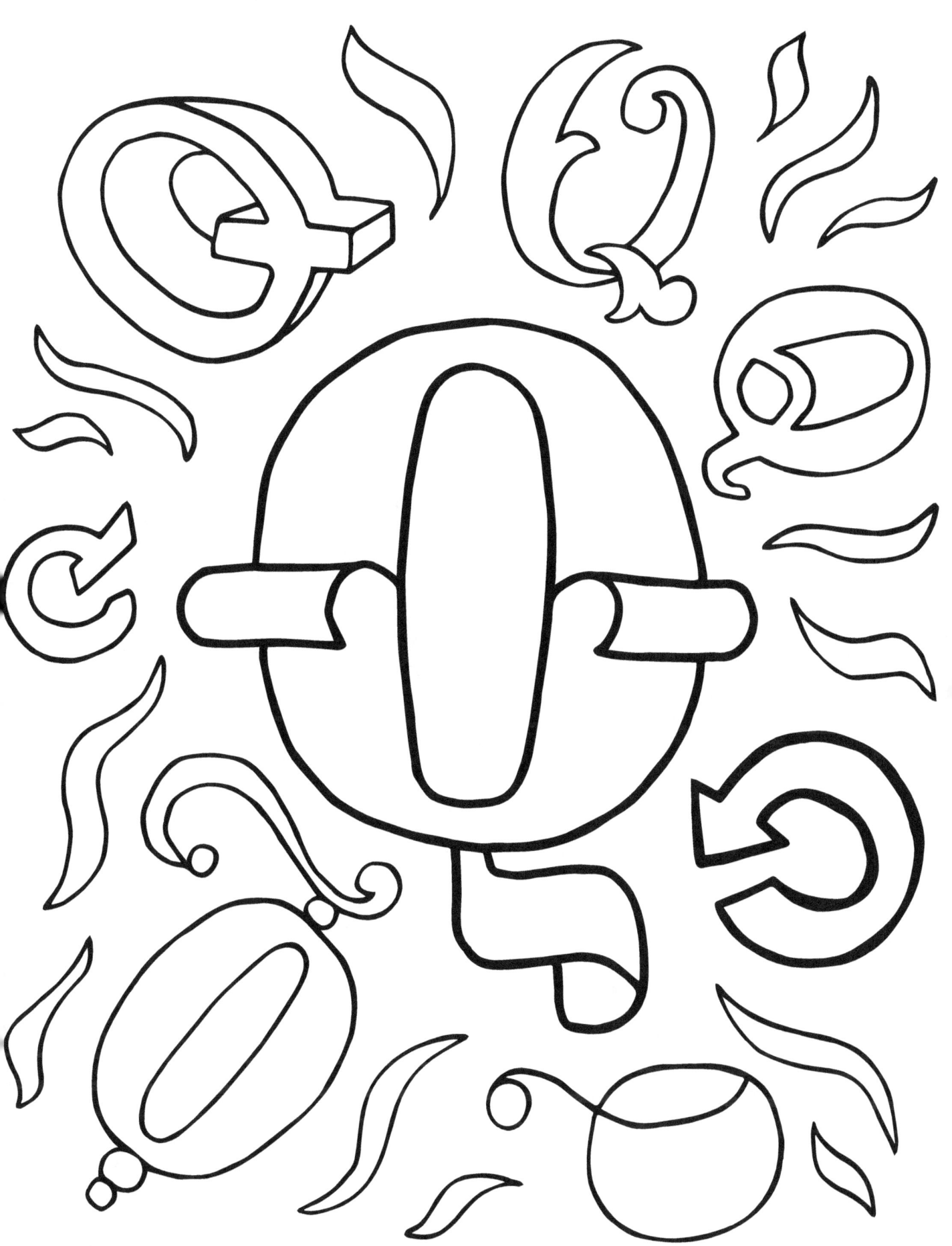

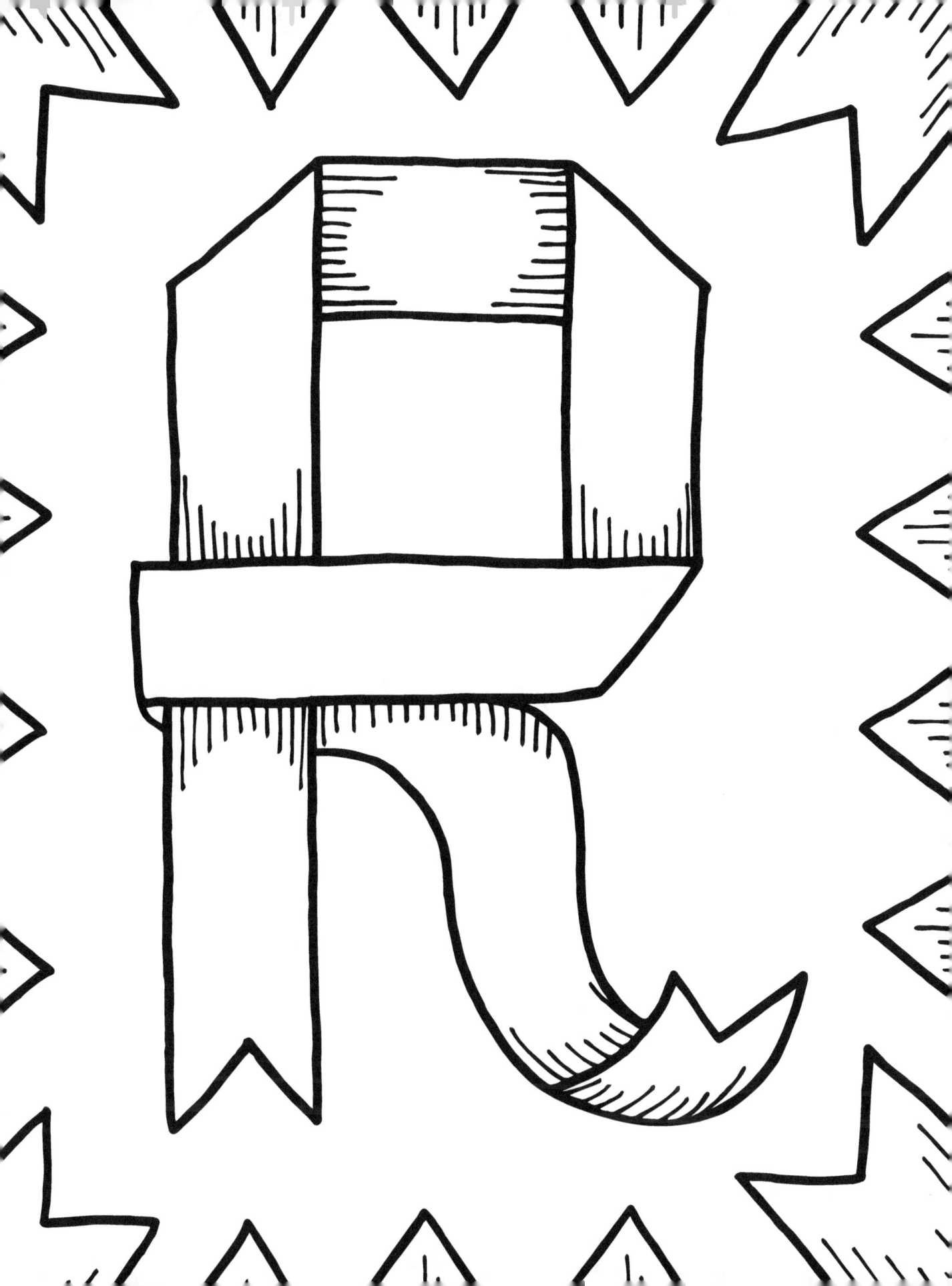

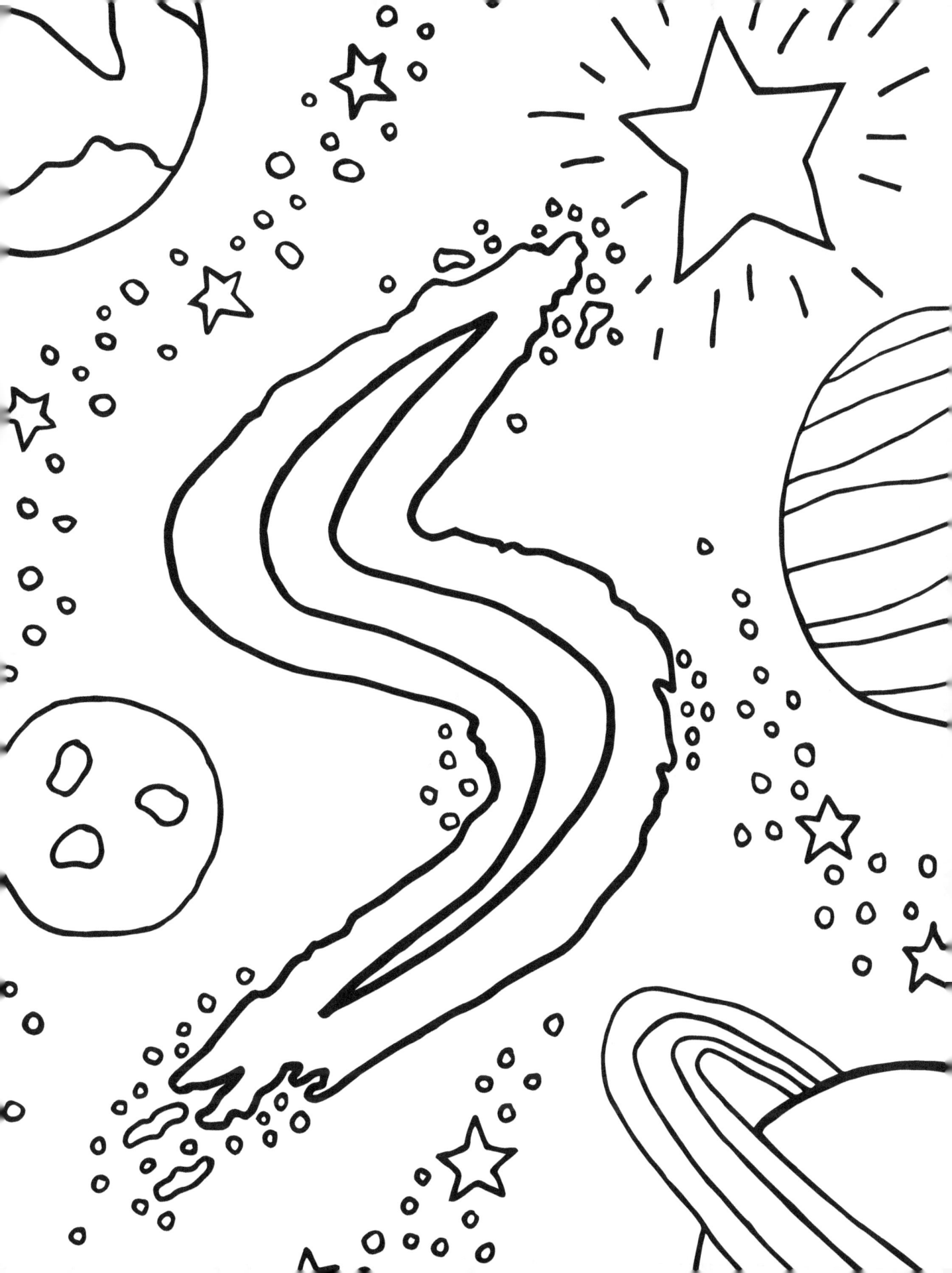

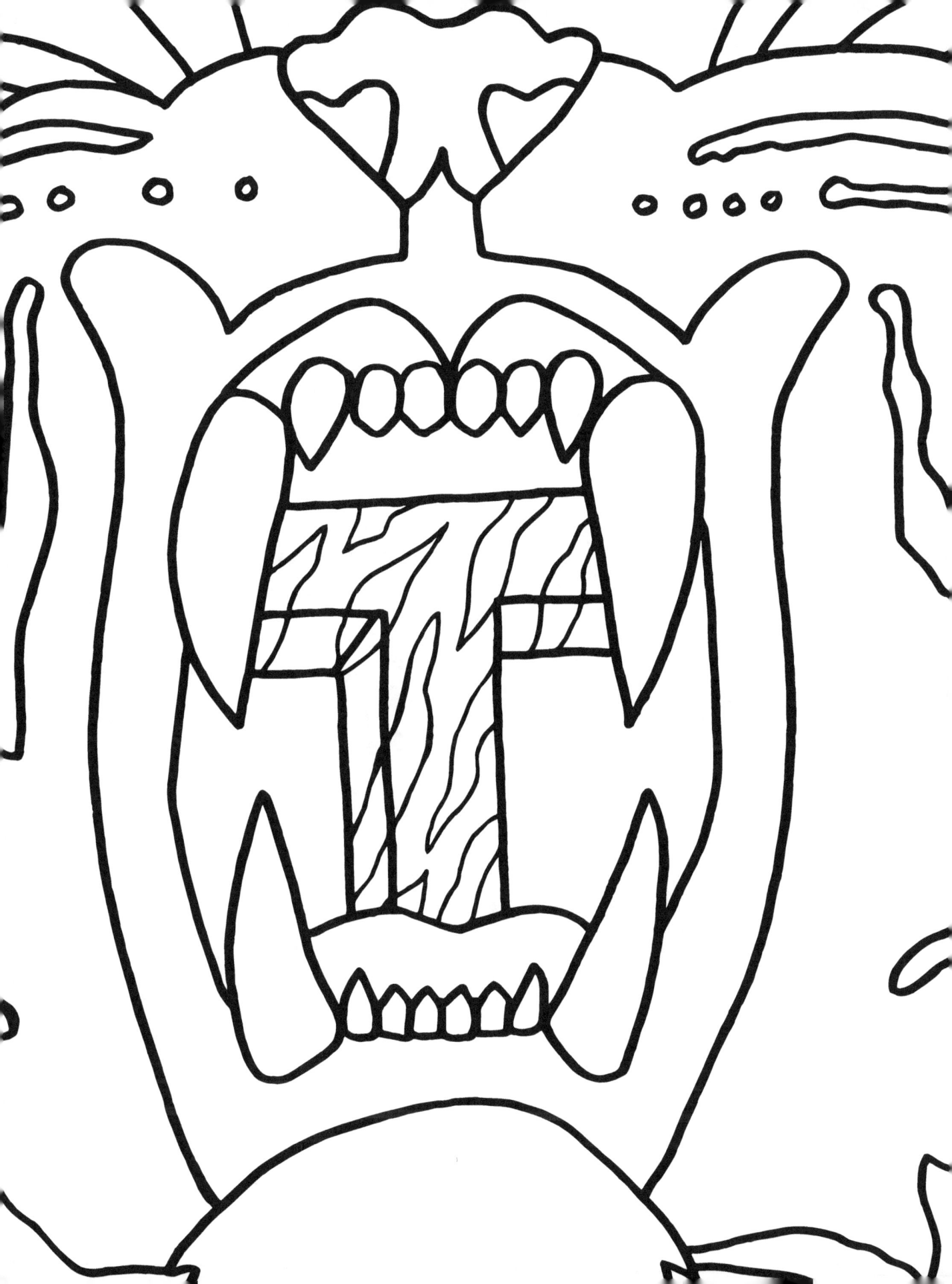

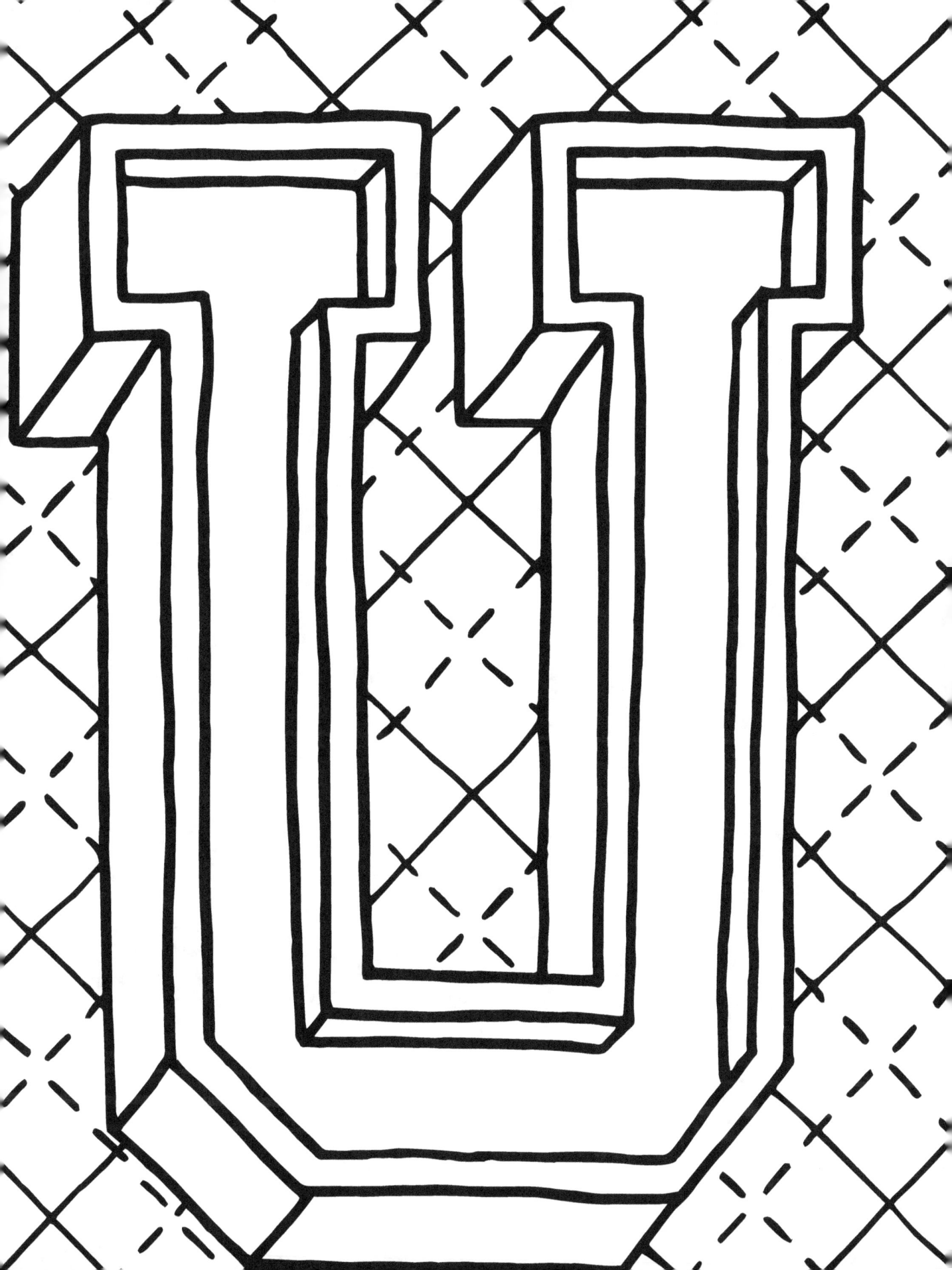

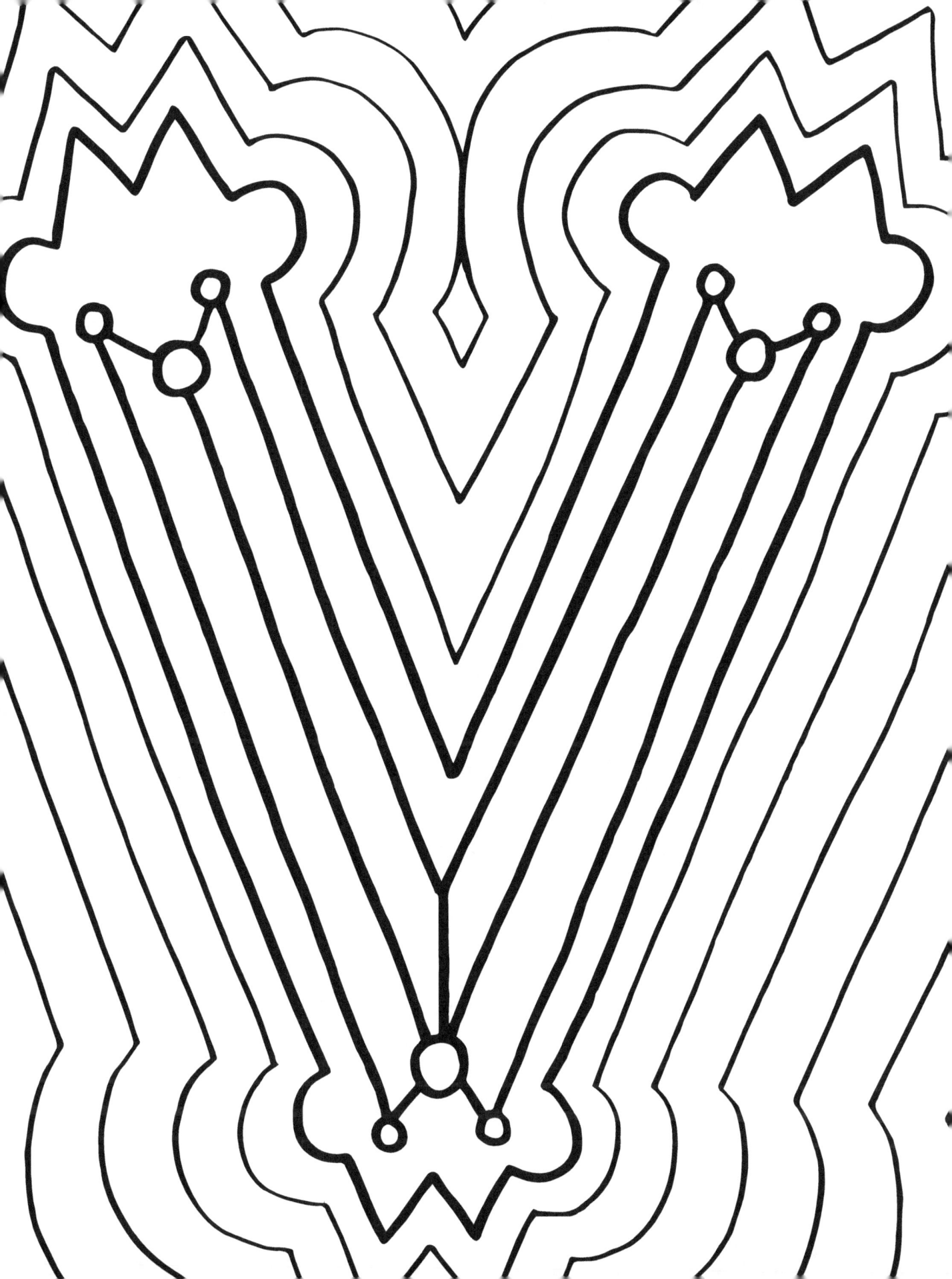

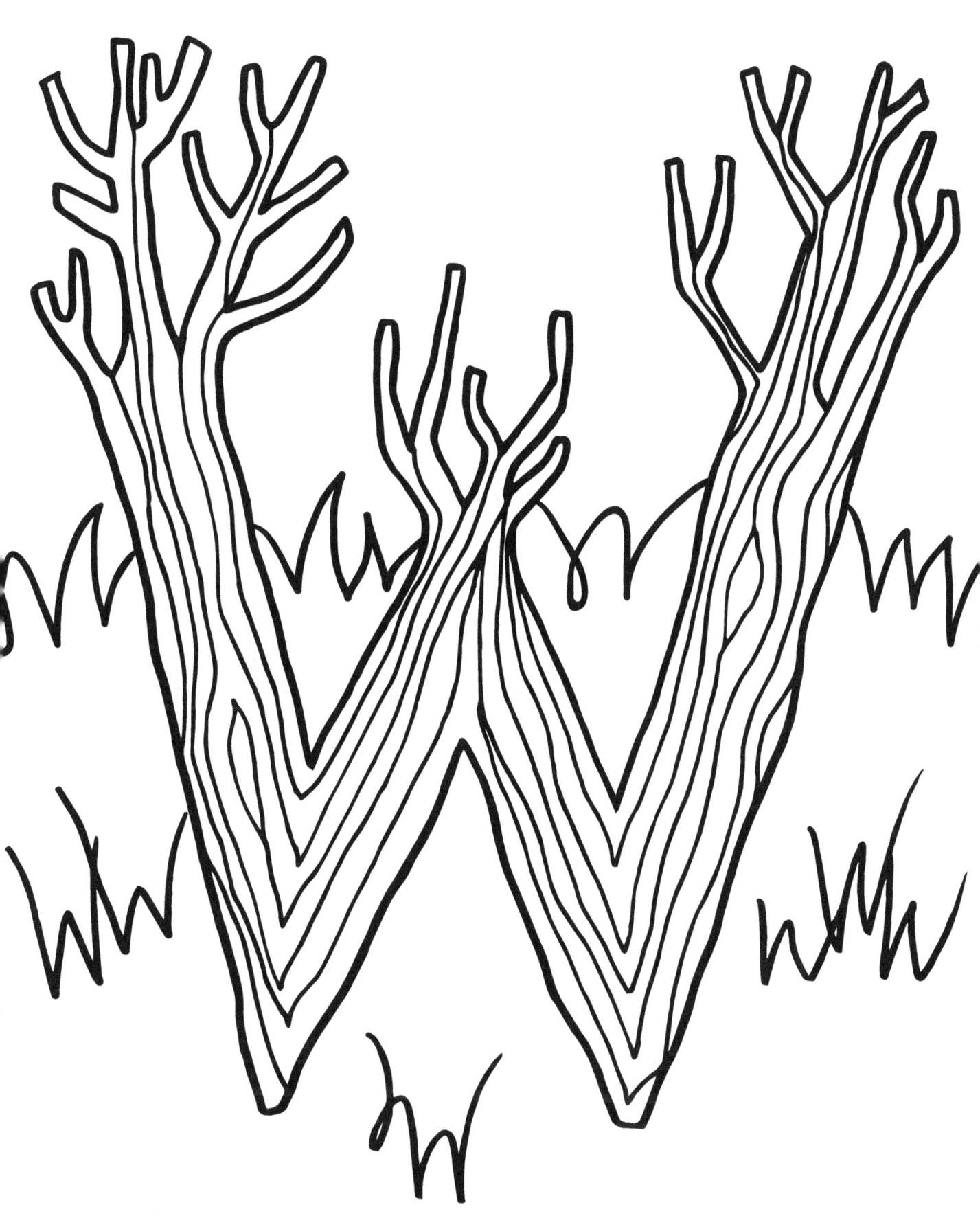

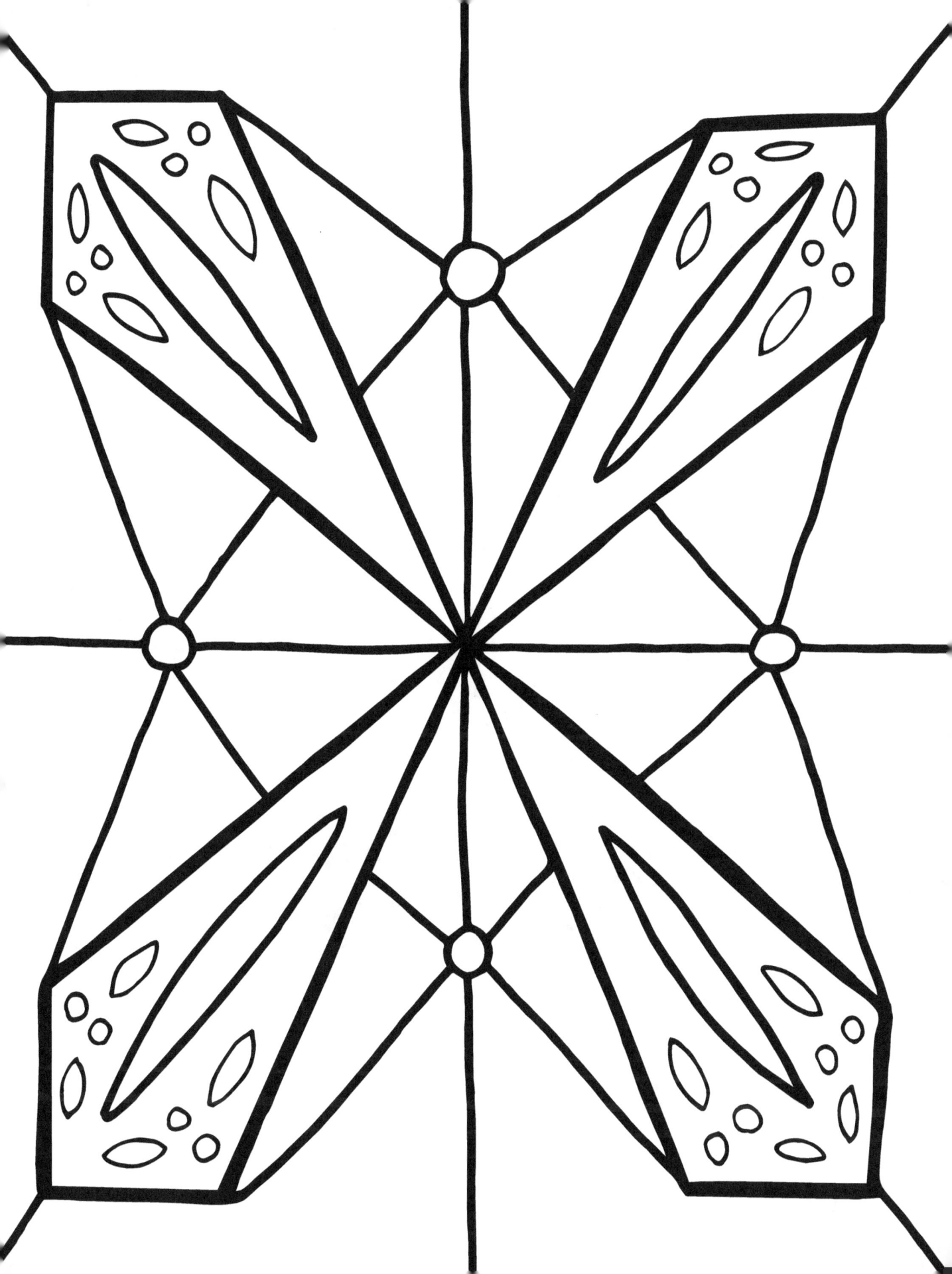

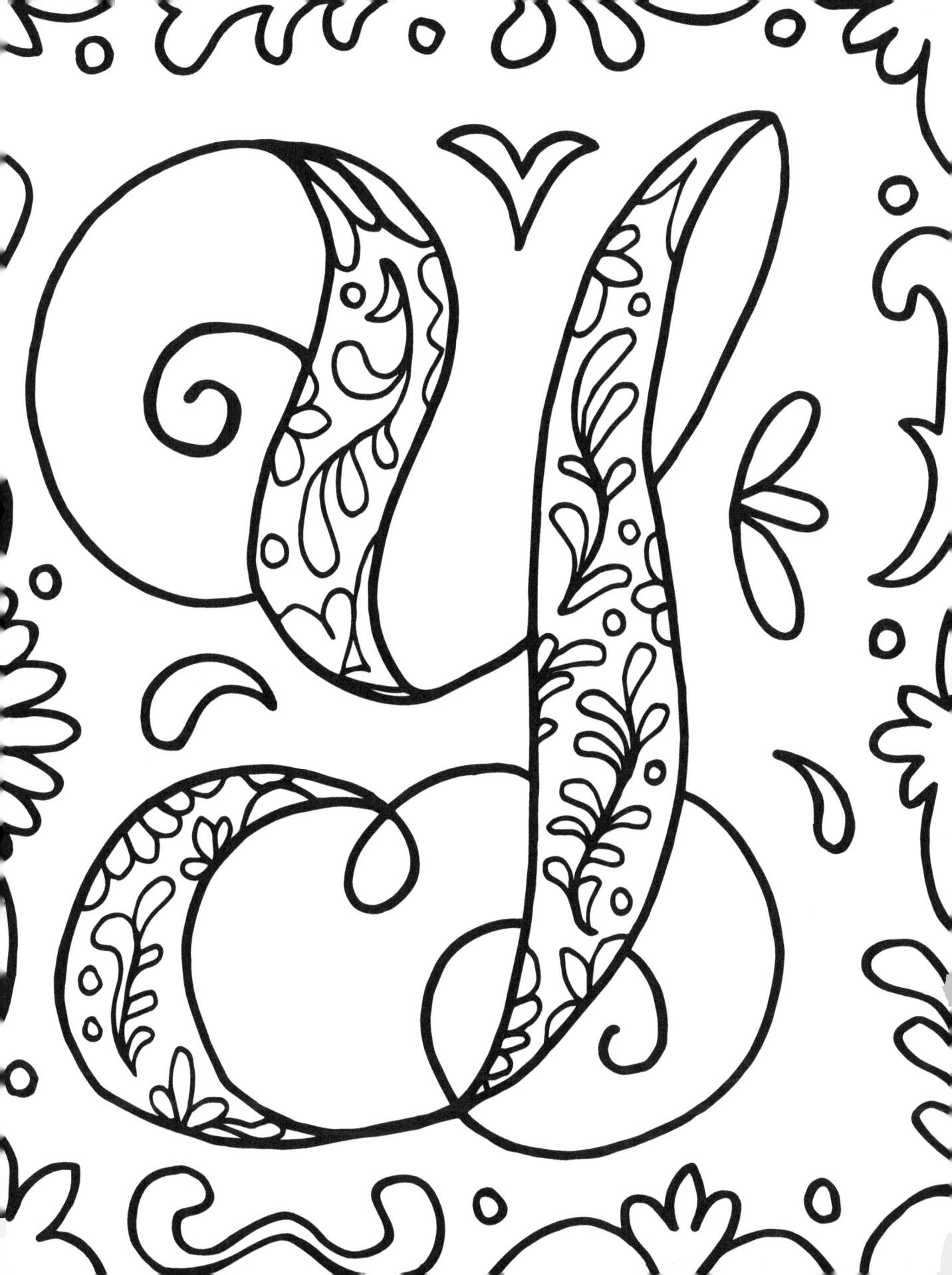

www.ingramcontent.com/pod-product-compliance
Lightning Source LLC
Chambersburg PA
CBHW081019170526
45158CB00010B/3097